T0224588

Model-Driven Development of Akoma Ntoso
Application Profiles

Amelie Flatt • Arne Langner • Olof Leps

Model-Driven Development of Akoma Ntoso Application Profiles

A Conceptual Framework for Model-Based Generation of XML Subschemas

 Springer

Amelie Flatt
Berlin, Germany

Arne Langner
Berlin, Germany

Olof Leps
Berlin, Germany

ISBN 978-3-031-14131-7   ISBN 978-3-031-14132-4   (eBook)
https://doi.org/10.1007/978-3-031-14132-4

This Springer imprint is published by the registered company Springer Nature Switzerland AG
The registered company address is: Gewerbestrasse 11, 6330 Cham, Switzerland

Someone's sitting in the shade today because someone planted a tree a long time ago.
   Warren Buffett

A smart model is a good model.
   Tyra Banks

Preface

Introducing machine-readability to a legislative system opens the door to a variety of exciting prospects from the world of parliamentary and legal informatics. For most legislative systems, it offers a chance to move away from a legislative cycle driven by paper and non- or only partially machine-readable documents and surpass all its associated shortfalls: Most legislative systems involve a number of different constitutional organs and bodies, as well as highly differentiated processes with numerous stages and decision points. Institutional handovers and stage changes are often marked by manual effort. This may include tasks such as correctly associating incoming drafts with their respective legislative efforts, transferring them into a given house style, and identifying changes that have been implemented further upstream in the process. Similar efforts can be involved in the analytical side of legislative drafting, where different versions of the same document may have to be analyzed and compared—sometimes even by using paper-based drafts. Additionally, references often have to be manually updated to account for changes that occurred during the drafting phase—changes that need to be noticed and pointed out by the editors. This can be exemplified by the need of many legal systems to regularly pass acts solely for the purpose of correcting false or outdated references or legal terminology. It can be particularly relevant when transposing supranational regulations into national law, e.g., in the EU. All of these manual tasks cause errors and oversights, leading to conflicting or faulty legislation and law, all the while slowing down the process of creating and maintaining law.[1]

The promise of legal and parliamentary informatics is to improve the speed and quality of legislative processes through machine-assisted drafting and machine-assisted (legal) analysis. The key to developing such tools is a machine-readable

---

[1] Bundesministerium des Innern, für Bau und Heimat, Projektgruppe Digitale Verwaltung (2020), Projektgruppe Gemeinsame IT des Bundes (2021c), Piesker et al. (2020), Bundesministerium des Innern, für Bau und Heimat, Projektgruppe Digitale Verwaltung 2020, Projektgruppe Gemeinsame IT des Bundes (2019b), Bundesministerium des Innern, für Bau und Heimat, Projektgruppe Digitale Verwaltung (2020), *Spezifikation LegalDocML.de—XML-Standard für Dokumente der Bundesrechtsetzung, Fassung vom 27.03.2020, Version 1.0.*

format for legislative documents on the basis of which these tools can operate and exchange information. Such a format also lays the foundation for future applications and use cases: Open data machine-readable and interlinked legal artifacts that go beyond mere legal texts but include parliamentary debates and amendments may give rise to new scientific, analytical, or even historical approaches, for example, in the social sciences or the legal field. Use cases such as the (partly) automatic structuring, evaluation, and comparison of legal arguments, rulesets, or legislation-linked smart contracts using rule representation tools will become possible based on aforementioned digitalization efforts. The full potential of these possibilities is yet to be explored.

With this outlook in mind, numerous countries and legal bodies such as the European Parliament, the European Commission, the EU Publication Office, the UK Parliament, the Scottish Parliament, the Italian Senate, the Parliament of Uruguay, the Library of Congress of Chile, the Official Journal of the Grand Duchy of Luxembourg, and the German federal executive bodies alongside the federal legislative journal as well as several agencies within the United Nations have initiated projects to digitalize their legislative systems by developing application profiles of the Akoma Ntoso (AKN) legislative document standard, which is to be used as a basis for such digitalization efforts.[2]

This book describes an approach to creating an AKN custom application profile and associated development methodology in detail, showcasing examples of the German legislative system, as Germany follows a corresponding approach in the creation of the German application profile of the Akoma Ntoso (AKN) legislative document standard under the name *LegalDocML.de*.[3]

It is intended as a practical guideline for teams preparing to create a custom application profile for their own domain. It thereby aims to fill the identified gap in the literature by providing a guideline for current and future development teams. The practical implementation of the methodology is exemplified in the context of the AKN ecosystem and, where applicable, the German legislative case that formed the basis for the methodology's initial development, but is usually abstracted or generalized as to be easily transferable to other use cases.

This book can serve as guidance to teams working on the numerous aforementioned and future projects. It provides readers with a comprehensive overview of the challenges we faced when developing and introducing an application profile of AKN. Furthermore, it can serve as both a resource and an inspiration for similar and yet to be developed methodologies in the public sector, in the health sector, or in defense, where international standardization and interoperability efforts are applied to a local level. The promising methodology demonstrated here presents possible solutions to these challenges.

---

[2] See, for example, AKN4EU by the Publications Office of the European Union, AKN4UN by the United Nations System, as well as the numerous other examples mentioned in, e.g., OASIS AKN and this book.

[3] Piesker et al. (2020, pp. 317); Bundesministerium des Innern, für Bau und Heimat (2020).

We deem this methodology a suitable approach to creating a custom application profile. Our paradigmatic analysis and description of the creation of a subschema-based application profile on the basis of the interoperable architecture and foundational development approach that we initially devised finds the presented methodology to be suitable for the development of application profiles. We are glad to report that the approach emphasized and described in this book has been successfully employed and is expanded upon by others: At the time of writing, the German application profile is being further developed. Tools for drafting, reviewing, and publishing legislation using this application profile are already in development. A number of German federal constitutional organs actively contribute to this effort and rightly see the standardized machine-readable representation of legislative documents as a key pillar of a digital legislative process.[4,5]

Berlin, Germany   Amelie Flatt
June 2022   Arne Langner
                                                                                                      Olof Leps

---

[4] Piesker et al. (2020, pp. 317); Bundesministerium des Innern, für Bau und Heimat (2020), Bundesministerium des Innern, für Bau und Heimat, Projektgruppe Digitale Verwaltung 2020, Projektgruppe Gemeinsame IT des Bundes (2021b), Bundesministerium des Innern, für Bau und Heimat, Projektgruppe Digitale Verwaltung (2020), Projektgruppe Gemeinsame IT des Bundes (2021a), Bundesministerium des Innern, für Bau und Heimat, Projektgruppe Digitale Verwaltung (2020), Projektgruppe Gemeinsame IT des Bundes (2021d).

[5] Any views or opinions represented in this book are the views of the authors and do not represent the people, institutions, or organizations that currently continue to develop LDML.de.

Management Summary

This book presents a model-driven approach to creating a national application profile of the international legislative document standard Akoma Ntoso (AKN). AKN is an XML-based document standard that serves as the basis for modern machine-readable and fully digital legislative and judicial processes. As such, it is designed to be suitable as a common exchange format in all parliamentary, legal, and judicial systems around the world. In order to support a wide range of legal documents and legal traditions, it offers an abundance of structural and semantic elements and combinations thereof.

Consequently, Akoma Ntoso needs to be adapted and specified for each use case by creating an application profile. While several approaches to designing and implementing such an application profile exist, the herein described model-driven development approach is advantageous because it ensures consistent and error-proof descriptive styles, even when using different software tools. It allows for easy maintenance, is self-documenting, and facilitates stakeholder validation with non-technical legal experts. The resulting application profile remains fully compliant to and compatible with Akoma Ntoso.

Beyond its abstract description, the development approach is paradigmatically applied to the German federal legislative process as a corresponding approach was used in the creation of the German application profile LegalDocML.de of AKN. We discuss how the methodology discussed in this book yields a model, schema definition, and specification that is corresponding to LegalDocML.de, using examples from Germany and the EU or that are abstracted or generalized as to be easily transferable to other use cases.

The herein described model-driven development approach is of interest to both legal and technical project teams on the cusp of introducing AKN in a legislative domain and intended as a practical guideline for teams preparing to create a custom application profile for their own domain. The resulting artifacts are fully AKN compliant, robust, and easy to maintain, in particular with respect to a heterogeneous IT landscape and long-term usage. The approach ensures an adequate consistency of legal documents while harnessing the sophistication of AKN. It is flexible enough to account for structural changes over time and allows for easy maintenance and adaptation.

This book is structured into the following sections:

Introduction describes the problem space and objective of this book and summarizes the methodology.

Background and Requirements details the need to create local application profiles and constraints encountered in light of AKN, exemplified by the German (federal) legal system, such as the organizational environment and complexity of drafting rules. It is against this backdrop that the section also features a brief excursion into the German application profile LegalDocML.de that is currently in development.

Phase 1: Mapping Legal Concepts to Technical Objects describes how a preliminary model is useful to capture collected requirements in a technology-neutral way and lists possible approaches to research, elicit, and structure requirements (such as top-down, bottom-up, and a hybrid of the two).

Phase 2: Formally Modeling the Domain and the Mapping shows how to turn this preliminary model into a fully formalized model. It investigates different model types and points out key modeling decisions that affect how specific requirements (such as contents and relationships of objects) can be represented and how the resulting model can be validated.

Phase 3: Generating Artifacts from the Model then explores how a fully formal model can be used to automatically generate the artifacts needed for the application profile (such as an XML schema and a specification document).

Outlook and Lessons Learned summarizes our analysis, namely, that the built-in extension mechanisms of AKN are best suited to specific and small-scale customizations and that the model-driven approach presented in this book works well for more extensive customizations. It then suggests that the model-driven approach can easily be applied to other, similar customizations of XML schema-based standards in other domains.

Contents

List of Abbreviations

AKN	Akoma Ntoso, Architecture for Knowledge-Oriented Management of African Normative Texts using Open Standards and Ontologies
AKN4EU	Akoma Ntoso for EU, a technical markup standard developed by the EU institutions that is based on Akoma Ntoso
AKN4UN	Akoma Ntoso for UN, a technical markup standard developed by the UN institutions that is based on Akoma Ntoso
JSS	Japanese Statutory Schema
LDML.de	LegalDocML.de, the German application profile of Akoma Ntoso
MDD	Model-driven development
OASIS	Organization for the Advancement of Structured Information Standards
OCL	Object Constraint Language
SVG	Scalable Vector Graphics
UML	Unified Modeling Language
VTL	Velocity Templating Language
XML	Extensible Markup Language
XOV	XML in der öffentlichen Verwaltung
XSD	XML Schema Definition
XSLT	Extensible Stylesheet Language Transformations

Chapter 1
Introduction

The OASIS standard Akoma Ntoso (AKN)[1] is an international XML document standard that specifies machine-readable representations of parliamentary, legislative, and judicial documents. It is rapidly becoming a key component of national and supranational efforts to digitalize legislative processes by providing a detailed, flexible, and intuitive vocabulary for XML markup of the said document types. Akoma Ntoso is not limited to data exchange within a single legislative, judicial, or administrative system. Instead, it aims to be compatible with most if not all such systems around the world and sets out to enable interoperable data exchange between these systems.

While this flexibility is advantageous for data exchange across multiple systems, it also creates the risk of ambiguous representations. This can create problems, in particular when documents are exchanged across several IT systems. Such inconsistencies can be avoided by defining rules and conventions on how AKN is to be used within a given legislative, judicial, or administrative system. These conventions can then be employed throughout the entire IT infrastructure.

Since the inception of AKN, numerous countries, such as Germany, as well as national and supranational bodies have decided to adopt AKN as the underlying data format for their respective efforts to digitalize their legislative system.[2] From

---

[1] Akoma Ntoso means "linked hearts" in the Akan language of West Africa and is an acronym for "Architecture for Knowledge-Oriented Management of African Normative Texts using Open Standards and Ontologies." While the correct citation of the standard is Akoma Ntoso (AKN), it is maintained and promoted by the OASIS LegalDocumentML (LegalDocML) Technical Committee (TC) and sometimes (erroneously) referred to as LegalDocML. It is pronounced "a-coma-in-toso." See also Dimyadi et al. (2017).

[2] In 2019, Germany decided to adopt AKN as the underlying data format for its project to digitalize the entire legislative lifecycle from drafting to publication under the title "LegalDocML.de." See Bundesministerium des Innern, für Bau und Heimat (2020), *Spezifikation LegalDocML.de—XML-Standard für Dokumente der Bundesrechtsetzung, Fassung vom 27.03.2020, Version 1.0*, p. 2, and Deutscher Bundestag (2020, p. 1). Also see http://egesetzgebung.bund.de/index_en.html and

legal drafting, over the legislative lifecycle, to eventual publication, legislation generally involves a set of processes with a multitude of often constitutionally and thus organizationally independent actors, each with their respective IT landscapes and tools. Given AKN's openness and flexibility, it is therefore necessary to develop a framework on the basis of AKN within which compatible usage and implementations are ensured amid these independent actors and heterogeneous software systems.[3]

There are several possible approaches to developing an AKN application profile, most prominently the AKN Subschema Generator,[4] but also hand-written Schematron rules or a hand-written XML schema. However, none of those fulfill the requirements of being able to enforce complex drafting rules and conventions, compatibility with the original AKN schema and documentation while maintaining consistency throughout the lifecycle of a document, as well as easy maintenance. These difficulties arise in particular when needing to reconcile complex structures of legislative documents with the internal logic of the XML schema defining AKN. Instead of the aforementioned development approaches, a model-based approach to developing an additional schema definition presents itself as a method that allows for the required complexity while ensuring consistency and compatibility with the original AKN schema. It is such an approach that also inspired the creation of LegalDocML.de.[5]

This book describes a methodology for a model-driven development approach to creating an application profile of AKN and exemplifies this methodology by showcasing examples of the German legislative system. The methodology involves the choice of a suitable mapping from legal concepts to AKN objects, followed by the documentation and validation of these choices with stakeholders and finally the development of a technical representation of the application profile. Akin to the German application profile that is currently in development and aims to ensure the required legal form and structure of legislative documents by making use of an XML data schema and Akoma Ntoso, the technical representation of the said methodology

---

http://egesetzgebung.bund.de/legaldocml.html. For a more comprehensive German description, see Piesker et al. (2020).

[3] On the need to adapt AKN to local customs, see, e.g., (Vergottini, 2018). More generally, see Organization for the Advancement of Structured Information Standards (2018), Akoma Ntoso Version 1.0 Part 1: XML Vocabulary. Edited by Monica Palmirani, Roger Sperberg, Grant Vergottini, and Fabio Vitali. 29 August 2018. OASIS Standard. http://docs.oasis-open.org/legaldocml/akncore/v1.0/os/part1-vocabulary/akn-core-v1.0-os-part1-vocabulary.html. Latest version: http://docs.oasis-open.org/legaldocml/akn-core/v1.0/akn-core-v1.0-part1-vocabulary.html, http://docs.oasis-open.org/legaldocml/. On the complexity in digitalizing legal systems, see, e.g., Piesker et al. (2020), for such considerations as exemplified by the German and EU legal systems.

[4] See http://akn.web.cs.unibo.it/akgenerator/.

[5] See Bundesministerium des Innern, für Bau und Heimat, Projektgruppe Digitale Verwaltung 2020, Projektgruppe Gemeinsame IT des Bundes (2021d), Bundesministerium des Innern, für Bau und Heimat, Projektgruppe Digitale Verwaltung 2020, Projektgruppe Gemeinsame IT des Bundes (2021c), Bundesministerium des Innern, für Bau und Heimat 2020. On the German XÖV toolchain that also uses a similar approach, see Büttner et al. (2014).

aims to achieve this by virtue of an XML schema against which documents marked up in accordance with the application profile are to be validated in addition to the original AKN schema.[6] This book is of interest to both legal and technical project teams on the cusp of introducing AKN in a legislative domain and facing similar methodology and design decisions. If a schematic representation of the domain already exists, this can be used as a starting point to employing the presented development approach, facilitating the early steps. As in the herein presented exemplary application to German federal legislation as well as the analyzed case of LegalDocML.de, such a schematic representation can be developed as part of the process.

After a brief overview of the challenge at hand, the methodology described in this book is centered on three distinct phases:

- Phase I: Mapping legal concepts to technical objects
- Phase II: Formally modeling the domain and its mapping to AKN
- Phase III: Generating artifacts from the mapping

We describe the starting point, objectives, inputs, and outputs of each phase and showcase examples from the analysis of the German federal legislative case study. We emphasize the creation of a mapping of legal concepts to AKN elements, its documentation and technical manifestation, and the generation of a specification document and of an XML schema. The possible use of naming and design rules as well as a maintenance handbook is briefly discussed. Finally, we present a brief evaluation of the discussed methodology as well as suggestions for further consideration and investigation.

In conclusion, the model-driven development approach is generally deemed well-suited to creating technical artifacts from the ground up and to generating derivative artifacts such as restrictive application profiles of existing artifacts. The resulting artifacts are fully AKN compliant, robust, and easy to maintain, in particular with respect to a heterogeneous IT landscape and long-term usage. The model-driven development approach ensures an adequate consistency of legal documents while harnessing the sophistication of AKN. It is flexible enough to account for structural changes over time and retains the advantage to manage odd structures, usage patterns, and other extensions of AKN.

---

[6] Bundesministerium des Innern, für Bau und Heimat, Projektgruppe Digitale Verwaltung 2020, Projektgruppe Gemeinsame IT des Bundes (2021d), Bundesministerium des Innern, für Bau und Heimat, Projektgruppe Digitale Verwaltung (2020).

Chapter 2
Model-Driven Development of AKN Application Profiles: Background and Requirements

Akoma Ntoso is an international legal document standard that serves as the basis for modern machine-readable and fully digital legislative and judicial processes. This is achieved by providing a coherent syntax and well-defined semantics to represent legal documents in a digital format. It is designed to be suitable as a common exchange format in all parliamentary, legal and judicial systems around the world.

Before diving deeper into the intricacies of the model-driven development approach to address this challenge, the following sections provide a general and more comprehensive introduction to Akoma Ntoso as well as a description of the background, challenges and requirements faced when introducing a local application profile, exemplified by the German federal legislative system. Furthermore, the section also features a brief excursion into the German application profile LegalDocML.de that is currently under development and uses a corresponding approach.

2.1 Akoma Ntoso: A Brief Overview

Development of the Akoma Ntoso document standard began in 2004 with the aim of describing parliamentary, legislative and judicial documents in a machine-readable format.

Taking advantage of the shared heritage present in all legal systems, Akoma Ntoso has been developed to have ample flexibility to respond to all the differences in texts, languages, and legal practices. Aiming to expand on certain common practices, the standard therefore has a broad scope. It provides, inter alia, a common extensible model for data (the document content) and metadata (such as bibliographic information and annotations). Specifically, as a common legal document standard for the interchange of legal documents it is designed to be highly

© The Author(s), under exclusive license to Springer Nature Switzerland AG 2022
A. Flatt et al., *Model-Driven Development of Akoma Ntoso Application Profiles*,
https://doi.org/10.1007/978-3-031-14132-4_2

flexible in its support of documents and functionalities,[1] maintaining a large set of both structural and semantic building blocks (over 500 entities in version 3.0) for representing this wide variety of document types of virtually all legal traditions.[2] It is extensible in order to allow for modifications to address the individual criteria of organisations or unique aspects of various legal practices and languages without sacrificing interoperability with other systems.

AKN was initially developed on the initiative of the United Nations Department of Economic and Social Affairs to encourage the adoption of digital technologies by African Parliaments in order to facilitate increased transparency and accountability. The project was later handed over to the LegalDocumentML Technical Committee (LegalDocML) of the OASIS standardization body, where it was further developed and ratified to become an official standard. Since then, it has been developed through the stewardship of OASIS and a worldwide community of practitioners. Akoma Ntoso is as such part of a wider approach to developing open, non-proprietary technical standards for structuring legal documents and information under the name of Legal XML, which also includes formats and standards for, e.g., eContracts, eNotarization, electronic court filings, the technical representation of legal norms and rules (LegalRuleML) or technical standards for the interfaces of, e.g., litigant portal exchange platforms.[3]

Akoma Ntoso allows machine-driven processes to operate on the syntactic and semantic components of digital parliamentary, judicial and legislative documents, thus facilitating the development of high-quality information resources.[4] It can substantially enhance the performance, accountability, quality and openness of parliamentary and legislative operations based on best practices and guidance through machine-assisted drafting and machine-assisted (legal) analysis. Embedded in the environment of the semantic web, it forms the basis for a heterogenous yet interoperable ecosystem, with which these tools can operate and communicate,

---

[1] Vitali and Palmirani (2019).

[2] Organization for the Advancement of Structured Information Standards (2018), *Akoma Ntoso Version 1.0 Part 1: XML Vocabulary. Edited by Monica Palmirani, Roger Sperberg, Grant Vergottini, and Fabio Vitali. 29 August 2018. OASIS Standard.* http://docs.oasis-open.org/legaldocml/akncore/v1.0/os/part1-vocabulary/akn-core-v1.0-os-part1-vocabulary.html. Latest version: http://docs.oasis-open.org/legaldocml/akn-core/v1.0/akn-core-v1.0-part1-vocabulary.html, http://docs.oasis-open.org/legaldocml/, section 2.1. See also Dimyadi et al. (2017), Sartor et al. (2011), Sartor (2016, p. 218), Boella et al. (2014, p. 173), Palmirani and Vitali (2012, pp. 159–169).

[3] Dolin (2021). Organization for the Advancement of Structured Information Standards (2019a), *Electronic Court Filing Version 5.0, Committee Specification 01, 18 April 2019,* https://docs.oasisopen.org/legalxml-courtfiling/, Organization for the Advancement of Structured Information Standards (2019b), *Litigant Portal Exchange Version 1.0, Committee Specification Draft 01 / Public Review Draft 01, 06 August 2019,* https://docs.oasis-open.org/lp/ Organization for the Advancement of Structured Information Standards (2021b), *LegalRuleML Core Specification Version 1.0, OASIS Standard, 30 August 2021,* http://docs.oasis-open.org/legalruleml/. Also see http://www.legalxml.org/.

[4] See for example Palmirani (2021), Sansone and Sperli (2022).

as well as for future applications and use cases based on digital law or rule representation.[5]

Akoma Ntoso is currently in the process of implementation or has already been implemented in various countries or supranational bodies: Aside from the German federal executive bodies as well as the German federal legislative journal, the list includes the European Parliament, the European Commission, the EU Publication Office, the UK Parliament, the Scottish Parliament, the Italian Senate, the Parliament of Uruguay, the Library of Congress of Chile and the Official Journal of the Grand Duchy of Luxembourg. Similarly, several agencies within the United Nations have initiated projects to digitalize their legislative systems by developing application profiles of AKN. Furthermore, it has also prototypically been considered for its usage in court documents, e.g., in Germany.[6]

2.2 Requirements for a Local Application Profile

AKNs universal scope and ambition, English nomenclature and structural flexibility may in many local applications not only be an advantage, but can also pose a challenge.[7] They carry the risks of diverging and, at worst, incompatible implementations by the independent actors along the legislative cycle: Legislative system such as in the EU or in Germany are usually characterized by a large variety of legally or factually independent constitutional actors and entities that each may implement the application profile in their own tools, which can pose a challenge. Similarly, they often do not use a standardized or uniform IT infrastructure.[8] The same often holds true for the digital publication of law: Different types of law may be published

---

[5] For a recent review of interoperable systems, tools and ontologies in legal informatics, see Loutsaris and Charalabidis (2020). For further examples specifically making use of Akoma Ntoso, see e.g. Stavropoulou et al. (2020), Moreno Schneider et al. (2022), Leventis Anastasiou and Fitsilis (2020), Palmirani et al. (2021), Joshi et al. (2021). However, also consider Francesconi (2022), for a discussion on the potential and limitations of the semantic web and related technologies such as AI in the context of legal informatics.

[6] See e.g. Publications Office of the European Union (2020), *Akoma Ntoso for EU (AKN4EU), Version 3.0*, http://publications.europa.eu/resource/dataset/akn4eu; United Nations System, Chief Executives Board for Coordination, High-Level Committee on Management (HLCM) (2020), *Akoma Ntoso for the United Nations System, Guidelines for the mark-up of UN normative, parliamentary and judicial documents*, https://www.w3id.org/un/schema/akn4un/; Vergottini (2018, p. 9), Ostendorff et al. (2020), Bundesministerium des Innern, für Bau und Heimat (2020).

[7] Gen et al. (2016).

[8] When looking at the German legislative system, Germany boasts a large variety of legally or factually independent constitutional actors and entities that each will need to implement the LDML.de application profile in their own tools, which can be particularly challenging. Specifically, the Office of the Federal President, the federal ministries, the Bundestag administration, the parliamentary committees, the parliamentary groups, the Bundesrat and the German states generally do not use a standardized or uniform IT infrastructure. In the EU, this is similarly the case as regards the European Council, the European Commission and European Parliament.

in different law or government gazettes, which may not only be comprised of one or more journals of legislative bodies, but sometimes even differ between executive bodies such as ministries.[9] Again, they each may have their own IT ecosystem built with the specific needs of the respective institution in mind.[10]

Therefore, when AKN is to be used in a local domain, it can be advisable to reduce the overall flexibility and complexity by specifying a uniform usage of a subset of AKN XML elements for the given use case.[11] In some legal systems, this is done via simply writing down a ruleset in a drafting manual and implementing it in a single tool used by all actors that guarantees uniformity and consistency in usage.[12]

However, as in the analyzed legislative cases, the complexities of a given legislative system and/or the heterogeneous IT landscape may instead result in the decision to augment the AKN schema with a technical codification of these constraints in an *application profile*. This codification primarily serves two functions. Firstly, it offers guidance for software implementation on how document structures and legal concepts are to be represented in AKN. Secondly, it allows for a formal way to validate AKN documents not only against the AKN specification but also against the national drafting rules applicable at a given point in time. A validated document would hence be fully compliant with AKN and with the codified national drafting rules. This combination of software implementation and validation against AKN allows legislators to easily draft legal documents fulfilling national drafting rules without having to be proficient in the underlying AKN standard, all the while ensuring the consistency and validity of the resulting AKN representation. Consequently, it comes as no surprise that Germany did in fact chose a similar approach and method with LegalDocML.de (see Sect. 2.3 for a brief description).[13]

The German case exemplifies how a consensus on how AKN is to be implemented in the various IT systems may need to be found and authoritatively documented. This consensus can be captured in a local application profile, which should generally cover the following aspects:

---

[9] In the German case study, executive law may not only be published by the Federal Law Gazette (Bundesgesetzblatt), but also by gazettes of the different federal ministries such as the Bundessteuerblatt (BStBl.) or the Gemeinsames Ministerialblatt (GMBl.). Similar examples are the Danish Lovtidende (Law Tidings) and Statstidende (State Tidings), which are respectively the law gazettes of the legislative and executive bodies.

[10] Piesker et al. (2020, pp. 317); Deutscher Bundestag (2020), Semsrott (2020), Heeger (2021).

[11] Sartor (2016, p. 283), Boella et al. (2015, p. 173).

[12] See for example the guidelines on AKN4UN: United Nations System, Chief Executives Board for Coordination, High-Level Committee on Management (HLCM) (2020), *Akoma Ntoso for the United Nations System, Guidelines for the mark-up of UN normative, parliamentary and judicial documents*, https://www.w3id.org/un/schema/akn4un/.

[13] Bundesministerium des Innern, für Bau und Heimat, Projektgruppe Digitale Verwaltung (2020), Projektgruppe Gemeinsame IT des Bundes (2021d), Bundesministerium des Innern, für Bau und Heimat (2020), Deutscher Bundestag (2020).

1. supported legal documents and their respective document structures, defined in a specification document and an XSD subschema,
2. the drafting guidelines in force at a given point in time, represented in a UML model, and
3. the mapping of legal concepts to AKN data types and elements, incorporated into the UML model.[14]

In addition, the following requirements for the creation of the application profile need to be taken into account: It should be possible to re-use constraints gathered in the application profile to support legislative drafting in editors and other implementations. Also, there should be a technical validation mechanism to test an editor's output against the application profile to ensure that all implementations are consistent and abide by the common ruleset. Furthermore, the application profile would have to be confirmed or approved by non-technical legal experts from the various bodies involved in the legislative process. Therefore, the application profile should be self-documenting to ensure coherence between the documentation and the codification of the agreed-upon usage of AKN. Finally, the application profile should be not only easy to maintain, but also fully compatible with and compliant to AKN itself. It should take into account the possibility of changes in drafting rules as well as changes to AKN over time. Consequently, the artifacts resulting from the herein described methodology suggest strict adherence to these criteria. A resulting subschema can be used for validation, allows for consistent re-use and application of a common ruleset, can be validated with stakeholders and experts and, finally, can be created via a model-driven development approach using UML-models as a single source for both the schema and the documentation.

Besides the herein presented development approach to creating an application profile, other technical approaches can be considered: Firstly, AKN comes with a dedicated tool, the Subschema Generator, to add custom structural rules to the AKN schema using XML Schema 1.1 assertions.[15] While useful, the authors find this purely technical output unsuitable for validation by non-technical stakeholders and not self-documenting. Furthermore, it is not deemed sufficient for the complexity of the existing drafting rules and conventions in some legislative systems, which is why other methods may need to be chosen. Secondly, the authors considered hand-written Schematron rules but point out that they suffer from the same drawbacks as the Subschema Generator.[16] Thirdly, a combination of written, domain-centric

---

[14] Unlike AKN itself, the herein described application profile does not aim to be universally and perpetually applicable, but rather, to formally capture (and make testable) a set of legislative rules at a given point in time. Changes in drafting guidelines over time would instead be addressed via a corresponding version of the applicable national application profile to ensure consistency and take into account changes over time.

[15] See http://akn.web.cs.unibo.it/akgenerator/.

[16] However, see the EU localization of AKN made use of this approach: Publications Office of the European Union (2020), *Akoma Ntoso for EU (AKN4EU), Version 3.0*, http://publications.europa.eu/resource/dataset/akn4eu.

documentation and a hand-written XML Schema represent another possibility. While this approach would be able to reflect the complexity of drafting rules and conventions, it is regarded as too error-prone and thus not recommended. Finally, a model-driven development approach is analyzed and determined suitable. The non-technical representation of all implemented rules can facilitate stakeholder validation and avoid errors, all the while allowing for the necessary complexity.

2.3   The German Application Profile LegalDocML.de

In 2019, as part of a project for the digitalization of legislative processes the German federal administration decided to adopt AKN as the underlying data format under the title "LegalDocML.de".[a] The project set out to digitalize the entire legislative lifecycle from drafting to publication, a set of processes involving a multitude of constitutionally and thus organizationally independent actors, each with their respective IT landscapes and tools. Given AKNs openness and flexibility, the project aimed to develop a framework within which compatible usage and implementations were ensured amid these independent actors.[b]

Currently, federal legislative processes in Germany are very much paper-based or only partially digital, with handovers or stage changes dominated by manual effort.[c] One result of an eventual completion of the German Akoma Ntoso application profile could be overcoming the downsides of a legislative cycle driven by paper and non- or only partially machine-readable documents with all its associated shortfalls. In its current state, German legislative drafting processes include such tasks as correctly associating incoming drafts with their respective legislative efforts, transferring them into a given house and/or stage style and identifying changes that have occurred further upstream in the process.[d] This is not trivial, as the German legislative system involves a number of different constitutional organs and bodies that are autonomous not only legally, but also with regards to their IT systems.[e] Similar efforts are involved in the analytical side of legislative drafting, where different versions of the same document have to be identified, marked and compared— sometimes even using paper-based drafts. Additionally, references have to be manually updated to account for changes that occurred during the drafting phase—changes that have to be noticed and pointed out by the editors.[f] This is exemplified by the regular passing of acts solely for the purpose of correcting false or outdated references or legal terminology.[g] All of these manual tasks cause errors and oversights, leading to conflicting or faulty legislation and law and slowing down the process of creating and maintaining law.

(continued)

In view of the above, the development of LegalDocML.de was started to do away with the unsatisfactory status quo in legislative drafting and to create an environment allowing for software-based improvements of the legislative processes. In 2019, the project showed via a prototypical approach both the viability of and support for the introduction of semantic technologies as a means of harnessing substantial efficiency gains in legislative processes via a wide-spread application of legal document standards, specifically LegalDocML.de.[h] Fundamentally, the German application profile could support legislative staff with functionalities that facilitate text-based work on a legislative document (for example automated conversions in accordance with a given template, automatic generation of synoptic comparisons as well as the creation of consolidated draft versions on the basis of comments and proposed amendments). Introducing machine-readability to the German legislative system could thereby open the door to a variety of exciting prospects from the world of parliamentary and legal informatics.[i]

Aforesaid evaluation was effectively a test of the suitability of Akoma Ntoso by means of a prototypical drafting of German legal documents in Akoma Ntoso XML, which was ultimately confirmed and formed the basis for a preliminary decision made on July 9th 2019 to further develop LegalDocML.de as the German localization of the Akoma Ntoso legislative document standard. For the framework within which to apply AKN to the German federal administration and legislative process, it was decided to create an application profile of AKN by essentially creating a model-driven subschema and specification; from its inception, LegalDocML.de was conceptualized and created by using a methodology that is fundamentally akin to the approach described and further refined in this book.

In this initial version LegalDocML.de covers draft bills in the form of laws, regulations and general administrative directives. As part of an ongoing development process, the standard could incrementally be expanded in future stages to include all relevant document types of parliamentary, legislative and promulgation processes and tools, as laid out in Bundesministerium des Innern, für Bau und Heimat, Projektgruppe Digitale Verwaltung (2020), Projektgruppe Gemeinsame IT des Bundes (2019b). The standard could also be expanded to include options for representation of the existing and historical legal body, which sometimes diverges from current drafting rules.[j]

---

[a]See http://egesetzgebung.bund.de/index_en.html and http://egesetzgebung.bund.de/legaldocml.html as well as Bundesministerium des Innern, für Bau und Heimat (2020), *Spezifikation LegalDocML.de—XML-Standard für Dokumente der Bundesrechtsetzung, Fassung vom 27.03.2020, Version 1.0.* For a more comprehensive German description see Piesker et al. (2020).

(continued)

[b]Bumke and Voßkuhle (2019, pp. 319); Piesker et al. (2020), Bundesministerium der Justiz (2022).

[c]Bundesministerium des Innern, für Bau und Heimat, Projektgruppe Digitale Verwaltung 2020, Projektgruppe Gemeinsame IT des Bundes (2021c), Piesker et al. (2020), Bundesministerium des Innern, für Bau und Heimat, Projektgruppe Digitale Verwaltung 2020, Projektgruppe Gemeinsame IT des Bundes (2019b).

[d]Piesker et al. (2020), Normenkontrollrat (2019)

[e]Piesker et al. (2020, p. 317), Bumke and Voßkuhle (2019)

[f]Piesker et al. (2020), Heeger (2021), Thieme and Raff (2017)

[g]See Kirchhof (2009, p. 43), and more generally Hamann (2014).

[h]Bundesministerium des Innern, für Bau und Heimat, Projektgruppe Digitale Verwaltung 2020, Projektgruppe Gemeinsame IT des Bundes (2019a), Bundesministerium des Innern, für Bau und Heimat (2020).

[i]Bundesministerium des Innern, für Bau und Heimat, Projektgruppe Digitale Verwaltung 2020, Projektgruppe Gemeinsame IT des Bundes (2019a), Bundesministerium des Innern, für Bau und Heimat (2020).

[j]Bundesministerium des Innern, für Bau und Heimat, Projektgruppe Digitale Verwaltung 2020, Projektgruppe Gemeinsame IT des Bundes (2019a), Deutscher Bundestag (2020).

Chapter 3
Phase I: Mapping Legal Concepts to Technical Objects

Having decided to adopt AKN, the first development phase aims to obtain a draft model of the domain, including a rudimentary mapping of legal objects (such as a typographical structure, a reference, or a signature) to AKN elements for each relevant document. Such a preliminary mapping mitigates the risk of utilizing ambiguous annotation and provides a starting point for further development. Ambiguity could arise because AKN "allows different document types to use the same names in completely different contexts and order."[1] It offers a wide variety of options in representing a semantic or structural component.[2] Akoma Ntoso rarely imposes limits on hierarchical structures or choice of AKN elements, which is why a document with a particular mandatory *legal* structure can be built in two or more different *technical* XML structures. While this would still lead to valid AKN markup, the ambiguity resulting from such variance could cause problems through unclear semantics and lack of interoperability, as different variants of markup are implemented and expected by applications along the legislative lifecycle of a given document.[3]

Therefore, a suitable markup needs to be found for every logical unit of a legislative document to ensure consistent use of AKN data types while remaining compatible with Akoma Ntoso.[4] These logical units can be grouped into different levels of abstraction, such as document components (e.g., cover page, legal text, justifications, and annexes), hierarchical elements (e.g., book, part, section, article, and paragraph), and content elements (e.g., text paragraphs, tables, and images).

---

[1] Vitali and Zeni (2007, p. 78).

[2] Akoma Ntoso is sometimes considered a framework, a collection of specifications, or a meta-standard instead of a sensu stricto document standard. See ibid., pp. 69–70, and Palmirani and Vitali (2011, p. 75).

[3] Gen et al. (2016).

[4] Vergottini (2018, p. 9). In particular, any valid instance of a specified AKN adaptation should be a valid instance of the original AKN.

A. Flatt et al., *Model-Driven Development of Akoma Ntoso Application Profiles*,
https://doi.org/10.1007/978-3-031-14132-4_3

Due to the variety and complexity of legislative documents, the mapping obtained in this phase is intended to be rudimentary: Its scope need not cover the full breadth of the domain, and its depth and modeling methodology need not be final. Instead, this first step's aim is to develop an understanding of how the domain-specific legal structures can be modeled in the available AKN constructs.[5] The initial mapping can be documented in several ways, for instance, in a detailed report, a tabular format, or a set of diagrams.

The definition of a preliminary mapping requires legislative and legal input. Virtually all jurisdictions offer some drafting guidelines or rules. In some jurisdictions, there may already be a formalized ruleset in the form of, for example, an XML rendition.[6] Other jurisdictions may only have general guidelines that are not as easy to translate into consistent and precise rule-based structures for building technical artifacts such as XML schemas. In this case, the existing guidelines first need to be formalized.

The process begins with a structured inventory of logical units or building blocks that are subsequently represented in AKN. It can be compiled using one of three approaches:

1. Top-down: In this approach, the inventory is deduced from drafting guidelines for specific document types and a logical taxonomy of their content.
2. Bottom-up: This inductive approach builds the inventory by sampling relevant documents and then structuring the findings.
3. Hybrid: The hybrid approach iterates between the top-down and the bottom-up approach. It uses a framework of formal rules derived from drafting guidelines to structure the various incarnations of building blocks as found in sample documents.

On the one hand, the top-down approach is a straightforward way of extracting written rules or guidelines for legal drafting, but it does not include implicit rules not codified in the said documents. The bottom-up approach, on the other hand, reveals structures encountered in legal practice: Legislative documents are analyzed in order to map all legal structures (e.g., titles, subtitles, articles, parts of document headers) to available corresponding elements and structures of Akoma Ntoso.[7] However, without detailed knowledge of formal rules, legislative processes, or guidelines, discovering these patterns, structures, and rules is time-intensive and prone to error. In the absence of an existing and formalized ruleset, we therefore suggest the hybrid approach, which is best suited to extract formally stated rules, while also addressing the challenge posed by hidden sources of requirements. This way, implicit drafting rules considered common practice within the domain can also be taken into account. Using the hybrid approach, these will become evident in the bottom-up analysis as

---

[5] Barabucci et al. (2011, p. 81).

[6] For example, Gen et al. (2016). On a more general note, see Palmirani and Brighi (2010).

[7] For a similar approach, see Koniaris Papastefanatos and Vassiliou (2016).

recurring patterns not originating from the drafting rules obtained from the earlier top-down phase.

Any kind of pre-existing structured data format used to represent documents within the domain can be used as a source for an inventory for the hybrid approach (e.g., the xNorm format and eNorm application in Germany,[8] Crown XML in the UK,[9] or JSS, the Japanese Statutory Schema[10]). The existence of such prior work simplifies the process of devising the initial mapping: Such a data format already identifies building blocks of a document, which can ideally be translated to AKN. Adjustments and additional design decisions will need to be made even in this case to take into account the structural differences between the pre-existing data format and AKN.

If, on the other hand, no suitable domain model is available as an inventory, the aforementioned hybrid strategy can be used as part of a prototypical markup experiment to conduct an inventory and draft a mapping. Such a strategy was successfully employed in the context of the German federal legislation.[11] For a prototypical markup to achieve that goal, a representative sample of relevant documents should be selected, grouped, and analyzed, taking into account variations of documents throughout their lifecycle. Second, each document's hierarchical outline is analytically broken down into self-contained parts that roughly correspond to AKN document elements, such as the document header, the main part, and a closing part. This breakdown facilitates the creation of an inventory. Thereafter, the documents and their respective outline and contents are modeled in AKN-valid XML instances as initial markup patterns. Rules and frameworks for the structure of the documents are frequently considered for guidance.

In the hybrid approach, different possibilities of representing legal information in Akoma Ntoso are tried out and compared. Ultimately, the aim is to find a way to model legal contents in Akoma Ntoso, which can be applied to all sample documents. Documenting the progress and changes in the mapping of legal structures of documents to Akoma Ntoso structures helps recognize and revise inconsistencies. An initial markup convention based on one sample document is applied to different documents to examine whether the chosen ruleset is consistently applicable. If not, the markup convention is adapted to be applicable to all priorly marked-up documents.

At this stage, it may not always be clear which markup option is best suited. In this case, it can be feasible to simply document the discrepancies between different markups and resolve them in phase II, in which a formal mapping is developed.

---

[8] See Bundesministerium des Innern, für Bau und Heimat, Projektgruppe Digitale Verwaltung (2020), for the XML-based data exchange standard, as well as https://www.enorm.bund.de for the Microsoft Word Plugin.

[9] Also known as CLML (Crown Legislation Markup Language); see, e.g., Boella et al. (2014).

[10] Gen et al. (2016).

[11] See, for instance, Bundesministerium des Innern, für Bau und Heimat, Projektgruppe Digitale Verwaltung 2020, Projektgruppe Gemeinsame IT des Bundes (2019a).

By considering different stages of a document's lifecycle, changes to a document throughout its lifecycle are taken into account while drafting and revising the markup. The preliminary model then becomes the foundation of a more elaborate formal model. This formal model, described in the next phase, aims to represent a consistent and complete domain model and AKN mapping.

The analysis of legislative system of Germany, but also of other legislative systems such as the EU, suggests the use of the hybrid approach, because despite the usual existence of (sometimes numerous) drafting guidelines and administrative regulations on legislative documents and processes, they often do not provide a sufficient level of detail and accuracy to deduce a ruleset suitable for the creation of an AKN application profile.[12]

For instance, drafting rules in a given legislative system may be explicitly laid down as optional but are nonetheless regarded as binding by legislative bodies.[13] Similarly, in other cases, rules may appear to be comprehensive but cover only the most common legislative cases (e.g., leave out rules on the drafting of laws that transpose international treaties into domestic law[14]) or contain inconsistencies as to the structure of legal documents and drafting rules when studied in detail.[15] In other cases, rules may be explicit, but formally binding only to certain legislative institutions (e.g., executive government bodies in a given legislative system), which results in uncertainty as to their applicability to other legislative bodies.[16] Therefore, opinions on the applicability of these rules in some jurisdictions may vary even among domain experts. Other requirements are purely implicit, such as requirements

---

[12] While, for example, the existing German drafting guidelines are rich in information, most lay down rules on the structure of legal documents either explicitly, but not in a sufficiently accurate and consistent manner, or implicitly (if at all), that is, without actually describing them.

The main guidelines and drafting rules for the German federal legislative system can be found in Handbuch der Rechtsförmlichkeit; Handbuch zur Vorbereitung von Rechts- und Verwaltungsvorschriften; Gesetz über die Verkündung von Rechtsverordnungen und Bekannt-machungen; Gemeinsame Geschäftsordnung der Bundesministerien (GGO); Geschäftsordnung der Bundesregierung (GOBReg); Geschäftsordnung des Deutschen Bundestages (GOBT); Geschäft-sordnung des Bundesrates (GOBR); and Geschäftsordnung für den Gemeinsamen Ausschuß (GemAusGO). However, adding to this, various internal rules and layout specifications as well as special provisions for specific legislative cases may apply.

[13] For an analysis of this example in Germany, see (Kahlert, 2014, p. 88). Conversely, the aforementioned binding rules are regarded as mere recommendations in Deutsch (2017, p. 104), and Thieme and Raff (2017, p. 403). See also (Weckerling-Wilhelm, 2013, p. 250).

[14] For instance, the German Manual for Drafting Legislation (HdR) primarily refers to the rather general "Guidelines on Drafting Ratifying Legislation and Statutory Instruments Relating to International Treaties" (RiVeVo) but does not cover the intricacies in drafting those legal instruments.

[15] On the ambiguities of German drafting practice as well as drafting rules, see Thieme and Raff (2017).

[16] For a respective German example, see Brunn (2004). He describes varying opinions in the parliamentary chambers about the applicability of such rules.

based on procedural rules that impact the structure of a document.[17] Also, older legal documents such as bills, which were passed into law decades ago when drafting rules differed from today's rules, have to be taken into consideration when taking inventory of the whole body of law.

Lastly, the question of how to deal with non-compliant documents should be considered: Due to the hierarchy of norms, the legislature may, for example, in times of political crisis, pass bills that do not adhere to drafting rules in content or form.[18] Therefore, even current legislation may be difficult to fit into a strict domain model, requiring a fundamental decision on how to deal with these structural edge cases.

---

[17] For example, different ways in which committees of the two German chambers of parliament, the Bundestag and the Bundesrat, deal with requests for amendments lead to differing parliamentary document structures. Compare, e.g., Bundestagsdrucksache 19/2741, https://dip21.bundestag.de/dip21/btd/19/027/1902741.pdf, and Bundesratsdrucksache 360/1/18, https://www.bundesrat.de/drs.html?id=360-1-18.

[18] Smeddinck (2013, p. 88).

Chapter 4
Phase II: Formally Modeling the Domain and the Mapping

Equipped with a preliminary domain model and marked-up sample documents, this phase aims to formally describe the domain and its mapping to AKN. The model and mapping developed in this phase should either be a complete and consistent description of the whole domain or a well-defined and extendable subset of the domain. In the latter case, other aspects of the domain or further information can be added incrementally. These properties allow the model to be used as the basis of a model-driven development process.[1] This approach offers several benefits, including consistency of all artifacts, reusability of the model regardless of the implementation technology, and easy stakeholder validation through the human-readable and domain-centric nature of the model itself. After systematic revision and improvement, this results in a consistent, logical, and advanced model that can serve as a basis for the development of software, XML schemas, and other technical artifacts that reflect the ruleset.

4.1 Step 1: Choosing a Format for the Model

Before formalizing the domain model and mapping, a suitable format needs to be chosen. This decision will affect most of the future lifecycle of the application profile of AKN. Ideally, this formal model should contain all relevant information on the use of AKN in the domain. This includes the allowed occurrences and combinations of legal objects, their mapping to AKN elements, as well as documentation and possibly references to rules, frameworks, and guidelines.

---

[1] In model-driven development, technical artifacts such as source code, documentation, tests, and more are generated algorithmically from a domain model. This approach was pioneered by early CASE (computer-aided software engineering) tools and further refined. See Beydeda et al. (2005).

A. Flatt et al., *Model-Driven Development of Akoma Ntoso Application Profiles*, https://doi.org/10.1007/978-3-031-14132-4_4

Specifically, the model is required to:

1. Define a complete and consistent mapping of legal objects or building blocks to AKN elements,
2. Depict properties of these legal objects and corresponding attributes of the AKN elements,
3. Represent relationships between legal objects and their corresponding AKN elements, depending on the context in which they occur,
4. Let information be extracted automatically into specification and documentation documents.

The model should be in a format that can be transformed into any of the artifacts mentioned above. The degree of representational complexity supported by the format strongly influences this consideration. For comparison's sake, three formats are considered:

(A) A table listing legal objects and their mapping to an AKN element or element combination;
(B) A graph depicting how the various legal objects and corresponding AKN elements are allowed to interact;
(C) A class diagram in which Unified Modeling Language (UML) describes the mapping of legal objects to AKN elements and relationships between them.

We will briefly compare these formats with regard to their specific suitability for model-driven development.

UML models (format C) and in particular UML models enriched with stereotypes[2] can be viewed as a graph (format B) with additional properties attached to both vertices and edges. Therefore, we will only compare our chosen format of a UML model to the alternative of a tabular description (format A). Instead of a UML model, any other graph-based structure, enriched by the necessary layers of information described above, could also be used. The mechanisms subsequently described in Sect. 2.2 could similarly be applied to such an enhanced graph. The main upsides of using UML are, firstly, the widespread and shared understanding of its specific syntax and semantics and, secondly, pre-existing infrastructure for creating and transforming UML models into other artifacts. The main upside of defining the structure directly on a graph is that the syntax can be explicitly chosen for AKN and the current use case. This frees the model from the constraints of the generic UML syntax.

Requirement 1 explicates the need to represent legal concepts as units within the model and assign them one or more corresponding technical elements from the AKN vocabulary. Legal concepts in this context are objects of hierarchy (such as a chapter, a paragraph, etc.) or content (such as a sentence, a reference, a list item, etc.). If there is a one-to-one mapping from legal building blocks to AKN elements that does not require complicated case differentiation, then a tabular description (format

---

[2] Object Management Group (2017, Sections 12.4.9 and 22).

A) is well-suited to fulfill requirement 1. For instance, legal objects can be listed row by row and matched to AKN objects. If there are case dependencies, it may be feasible to use a tabular description, though adequate case descriptions need to be found. However, with increasing complexity, a tabular representation will eventually cease to be human-readable and become overloaded with additional information required to capture all eventualities and combinations of scenarios. In contrast, a UML model would see legal concepts represented by UML class objects, while several mechanisms provided by the language can be used to capture corresponding AKN elements.

Our research showed that the default UML class diagram objects are insufficient to depict all legal objects, their interdependencies, and their mapping to AKN. Additional layers of information are required. To this end, custom UML stereotypes can be added for these supplementary layers. For example, basic UML vocabulary can be used to formalize the legal domain, while custom stereotypes define the mapping to AKN. Stereotypes can also be used to depict additional facets of the connection between several legal or legal and AKN objects or to add documentation to individual objects. This also allows the assignment of one or more AKN elements to a legal object in a specific context. Introducing custom stereotypes increases the complexity of the model but is nevertheless advantageous: All mapping information is contained in the UML class of a legal object, and the basic UML vocabulary can be used solely for defining relationships between legal objects. In contrast, the two dimensions of a regular table are exhausted by the mapping in the tabular definition.

Requirement 2 is concerned with the description of properties of legal objects within the model and their mapping to attributes of AKN elements. These can be added to both the tabular description, for example, by adding another column, and the UML model, by adding UML attributes to the UML class representing the legal object or to the stereotype corresponding to the AKN element. Therefore, requirement 2 does not yield a preferred choice of format.

Requirement 3 posits the need for the model to express complex relationships between entities. These relationships entail dependencies across multiple layers of the hierarchy, such as mandatory content elements resulting from a particular document type. For example, the model might have to express that a certain type of bill must contain a mandatory formula as a "great-grandchild" in the XML document. Representing such constraints is a nontrivial requirement. When trying to represent these complicated, multi-level relationships of logical units in legal documents in a table, it becomes evident that legal documents intrinsically carry a graph-like structure. Depending on where in a legal document a particular combination of legal objects is encountered, different rules apply to its "neighboring" legal objects, that is, objects on the same hierarchical level, and its "child" legal objects, that is, objects that are nested into the current object. Similarly, an AKN instance, as a XML document, effectively takes the form of a tree structure. Therefore, it is clear that a graph-like structure is much better suited to meet requirement 3. The varying relationships between different objects such as logical conjunctions or disjunctions, as well as different multiplicities, require not just simple vertices and edges in a graph but can be depicted through the many different types of associations available in UML.

Regarding requirement 4, a UML-based description is advantageous: In order to automatically extract information from our model and use it to generate artifacts, the model needs to follow computer-interpretable rules. In a tabular description, differentiation between cases is a priori text-based. To allow for automatic extraction of information, strict rules need to be imposed on the natural language used for case descriptions, and a corresponding interpreter needs to be written. This process is cumbersome and error-prone. In UML, on the other hand, all definitions of classes, properties, attributes, stereotypes, and associations are formally defined, following strict rules. Furthermore, several interpreters of UML into other formats such as XML schema or text-based documentation already exist, which can be reused or adapted.

At this stage, no decision on modeling technology or future artifacts is necessary. However, it is advisable to take into account which technologies might be used to incorporate all necessary data into the formal model. Taking into account how technical artifacts could be generated automatically from a formal model helps to highlight which details need to be modeled. Therefore, we recommend looking ahead to phase III while designing the formal model.

4.2 Step 2: Designing the Formal Model

This subsection is concerned with logical structures that have to be considered when designing the formal model. As discussed in Sect. 4.2.1, legal documents are structured similar to directed graphs and can hence be modeled as a directed graph, enhanced by several logical structures. Before defining the formal model, design rules need to be formulated to ensure consistent modeling. To this end, frequent structures in legal documents such as multiplicities, orders, nested structures, and less apparent structures such as dependencies over several hierarchical levels are identified. The structures discussed here will be demonstrated in UML but can be modeled in any enhanced graph, as mentioned in Sect. 4.2.1.

4.2.1 Basic Logical Operators

Any legal domain contains concepts corresponding to the basic logical operators of conjunction and disjunction (both inclusive and exclusive). For example, in the German legislative system, bills always need to consist of a preamble, a main part, and a closing formula, but can, within the main part, contain only articles *or* only paragraphs (which may themselves be further divided into logical substructures).[3]

---

[3] See Bundesministerium der Justiz (2008) *Handbuch der Rechtsförmlichkeit, 3. Auflage*, Bundesministerium der Justiz, URL: https://hdr.bmj.de/.

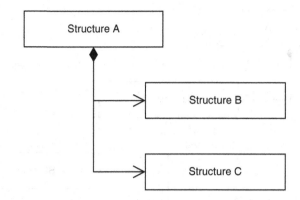

Fig. 4.1 Sample conjunction

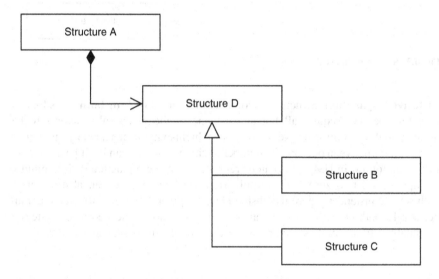

Fig. 4.2 Sample exclusive disjunction

Conjunction Structure A contains structures B **and** C. Not only two, but any number of structures can be given as part of a conjunction, meaning that each of them has to appear as a substructure (see Fig. 4.1). It is important to realize that a single legal element does not necessarily suffice to describe substructures, which often contain complex substructures themselves. We therefore refer to legal structures and not elements. In UML, we use navigable associations to depict conjunctions.

Exclusive Disjunction Structure A contains structure B **or** C but **not both**. This logical operator requires exactly one of the given structures to follow, but any number of choices can be given (see Fig. 4.2). In UML, we use generalizations to depict exclusive disjunctions.

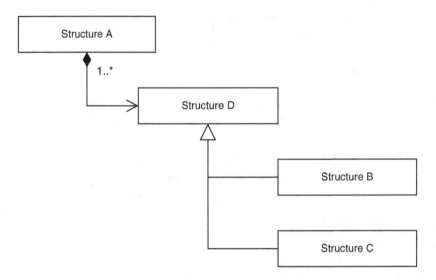

Fig. 4.3 Sample inclusive disjunction

Inclusive Disjunction Structure A contains structure B **or** C **or both**. This logical operator does not require all but at least one of the given substructures to be nested into the current structure (see Fig. 4.3). Inclusivity means that any number of substructures between one and the number of choices (which can itself be arbitrarily large) can follow. In UML, this can be represented by a conjunction with minimum multiplicities set to zero (for multiplicities, see below) or by an abstract class with several instances where the abstract class is given a multiplicity (see diagram below). In both cases, an additional layer of restriction is needed to exclude the eventualities of an empty structure or repeated equal structures, respectively.

4.2.2 Orderings

Both conjunctions and inclusive disjunctions can require an ordering of the nested structures or not. An ordered conjunction can be understood as an ordered sequence. This means that the given substructures all have to appear in a given order. In case of an inclusive disjunction, some structures can be left out of the ordered sequence, but all appearing substructures still need to maintain the given order.

4.2.3 Multiplicities

Legal structures frequently have a prescribed number of occurrences. For example, an introduction or conclusion might only be allowed to appear once, whereas there might be a minimum of two articles in a specific type of bill. Associations in UML can be equipped with multiplicities, giving an easy way to incorporate multiplicities in conjunctions and inclusive disjunctions. UML generalizations themselves cannot be equipped with multiplicities; hence, the multiplicities need to be encoded in the substructure itself, that is, in the substructures of the substructure. For example, a paragraph can optionally contain numbers, but if it contains any, it must contain at least two. We need to introduce the structures of `paragraph_content` representing a paragraph without numbers and `paragraph_numbers` representing a paragraph with numbers. The structure `paragraph_numbers` then has an association to the structure `number` with a minimum multiplicity of two.

To increase readability, consistency, reusability, and maintenance of the model, a modular model structure is recommended. It is advisable to package several legal structures into a larger structure whenever possible. For instance, in the example of a paragraph that can either contain content or numbers, we advise defining the structure `paragraph` as an exclusive disjunction of `paragraph_content` and `paragraph_numbers` (in UML, this is a class `paragraph` with two specializations). This structure `paragraph` will then be mapped to the AKN element `paragraph`.

4.2.4 Dependencies over Several Hierarchical Levels

A feature of legal domains is that legal elements or structures can impact other structures much deeper in the document tree. For example, the type of legal document chosen at the very root of the document may affect the types of preambles or closing formulas permitted or required at a deeper-nested position, for instance, in the main part of a bill. Formally representing these multi-level constraints in a model is challenging, and so is enforcing them in a schema file, as both can drastically increase complexity. One solution is to add these constraints as assertions to an XML Schema Definition, using assertions in XSD 1.1 or Schematron assertions.

Alternatively, these can be included in the application profile as rules expressed in natural language. As such, these rules are not technically enforced on the schema level but can still be mandated by the standard, e.g., in its specification, requiring them to be considered in implementations. Given the risk of ambiguities and their lack of technical enforcement through validation rules, these dependencies should be used sparingly. However, even though they would not be included in the schema, they can still be captured in the domain model (e.g., as part of a UML stereotype) and automatically be included in relevant places of the specification document.

4.2.5   Documenting Modeling Rules

Modeling rules need to be documented to ensure consistent use of the chosen modeling rules and their intended transformation mechanisms. This can be done by specifying for each logical operator its corresponding depiction in UML and its generated result in XML schema as well as any other generated artifact. Furthermore, specific stereotypes reserved for documentation can be used to add documentation to legal structures or rules, for example, giving a reference to a legal basis or a drafting guideline.

4.2.6   An Example Formal Model

This section describes an exemplary formal model using the previously described structures. The formal model was designed as to be able to reflect the complexity of legislative systems such as the German one, which by virtue of its complexity as well as its own application profile again serves as a superb illustration.[4] As discussed above, intricate and particularly specific constraints on the structure of legislative documents, such as those governing the drafting of German federal legislation, can be mirrored in the customization of AKN by building a separate, stricter XML schema using AKN data types. Based on prior experience with model-driven design from the XÖV category of German public administration XML data exchange standards, the authors similarly recommend using UML as a modeling language for the formal model.[5] This allows for a representation of domain structures using class diagrams, which can then be translated into data structures in an XML schema.

In these class diagrams, classes are chosen to represent the legal structures that make up the structure and content of legislative documents. The logical connections between legal structures are represented using compositions and multiplicities to signify nesting ("*structure A* contains *n* structures of *type B*") and generalizations to signify alternative occurrences of the same concept ("*structure A* can occur either as *variant B* or *variant C*"). Classes and their relationships are appropriately grouped into UML packages to modularize the UML model. The formal model for legislative documents is constructed using just these UML concepts.

A custom stereotype is added to the model for documentation (see Fig. 4.4). Tags are assigned to the stereotype to hold information on the legal basis and a short description of legal structures. A Boolean value is added to indicate whether the structure in question is an actual domain structure or a technical structure required by the modeling guidelines. This also allows for the generation of a simplified

---

[4] For a discussion on this complexity, see, e.g., Waltl and Matthes (2014), who look at it from an information systems engineering perspective.

[5] Büttner et al. (2014). For a more recent German elaboration on the importance of this approach for the digitalization of the German public administration, see Döring and Noack (2020).

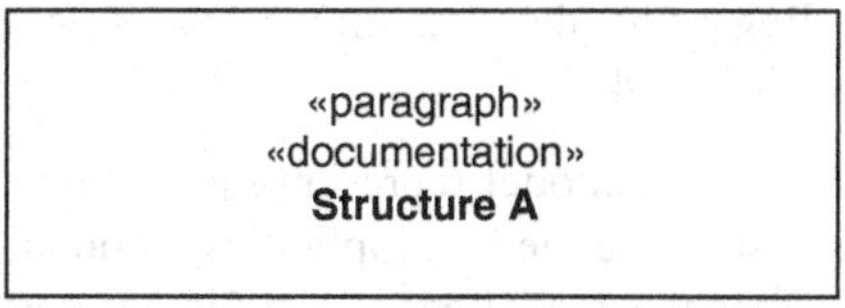

Fig. 4.4 Sample notation for a legal structure mapped to a paragraph in AKN with an added stereotype for documentation

«paragraph»
«documentation»
Structure A

Table 4.1 Overview of UML object notation for AKN data types

AKN aspect	UML construct
Complex type	Class
Element	Stereotype
Content element	Class property type
Multiplicity of content element	Relationship multiplicity
Attribute	Stereotype property (tag)
Documentation	Custom documentation stereotype

version and visualization of the model containing only domain structures. Reducing complexity, this facilitates the validation of the model with domain experts.

Next, the model objects are mapped to AKN elements. The entirety of elements from the original AKN XML schema is imported into the model as UML stereotypes and their attributes as corresponding tags. These are then used to annotate the model content, thereby assigning AKN elements to the UML class of each legal object (Table 4.1).

The assignment of a single stereotype to a class represents a direct mapping: The object's content is wrapped into AKN tags corresponding to the stereotype. Multiple assigned stereotypes corresponded to a combination of nested tags, based on the order of stereotype assignment. Helper classes included for reasons of model consistency (such as placeholders for multiple alternative structures) would not necessarily be assigned a stereotype at all, as these would never be instantiated or directly mapped to AKN elements.

This model design is then used to model an initial sample of documents and content, focusing on a small selection of high-level document structures and a few common constellations of lower-level hierarchical elements and their relationships.

4.3   Step 3: Checking the Formal Model for Consistency and Correctness

Being the driving input of this development process, the quality of the model is a decisive determinant of all outputs derived from it. Consequently, we are most interested in two dimensions of model quality: firstly, the correctness of its content, that is, its fidelity in representing the domain, and, secondly, its internal consistency, meaning its adherence to modeling rules.

Regarding the first dimension of model quality—correctness—two questions should be asked:

- Does the model represent the domain accurately regarding structures and their nesting, defined multiplicities, optional contents, and documentation?
- Does the model cover a sufficient portion of the domain, thereby fulfilling the scope required?

The first question can be refined to inquire whether the relevant structures of all legislative documents under consideration are present in the model and whether their relationships in the model reflect the real-world relationship within the domain. The second question can be concretized to assess whether the model covers all the documents required at this development stage.

To investigate these questions, quality management can target both the model itself and the outputs generated from it. To validate the model itself, subject matter experts (often domain stakeholders) will have to evaluate and validate the model using one or more of the following methods:

- A model walkthrough: a narrated, possibly interactive presentation of the entire model;
- Aspect-specific alternative artifacts to showcase individual facets of the model such as visualizations, simplified UML, overview tables, and the like;
- Independent inspection by subject matter experts.

To validate the model based on its outputs, technical experts need to determine whether the technical artifacts are a valid representation of the domain as required by the technical environment in which the artifacts are to be used. For example, a schema intended to validate documents should demonstrably work with the parsers available to the applications using the documents.

Findings from validating the model and its outputs must be reviewed before being fed back into the model development process. If the refined requirements adhere to the modeling methodology, they can be included directly in the model itself. They might, however, require changes to the modeling logic and artifact generation.

The second dimension of model quality—consistency—demands that the model complies with modeling rules. It ensures a predictable input to the subsequent development steps. The fundamental interest is to prevent unexpected side effects while generating artifacts that result from unexpected content and content constellations in the model. A consistent model reduces complexity in the generation process and, later, implementation. Consequently, this dimension can be investigated along a single guiding question: Does the entire model adhere to all modeling rules set down in phase II of the development process?

Again, this question can be answered based on both the model and the outputs generated from it.

Ex ante validation of the model can focus on the model's fidelity with regard to the following three rulesets, all of which can be checked by the project team itself:

- Specifications of the modeling language used (such as the UML specification);[6]
- Custom modeling rules and methodology, as defined in the development process;[7]
- Naming and design rules, as committed to by the project team and stakeholders.

Ex-post validation of generated artifacts serves to detect anomalies in the output that hint at inconsistencies in the model. Artifacts can be checked for unexpected content or validated using a specific validation method, such as schema validation for XML-based outputs, or linting and static code analysis for boilerplate code artifacts. Furthermore, technical experts from the expected usage environment can be invited to assess the technical artifacts' suitability and notify the development team of inconsistencies.

---

[6] Dedicated modeling tools commonly offer integrated model validation against these specifications, for example, MagicDraw, Rational Software Architect, Simulink, and Sirius.

[7] Custom rules can be captured and tested against using a wide variety of pattern- and rule-based languages, such as OCL (Object Constraint Language) and XSLT (Extensible Stylesheet Language Transformations), which many dedicated modeling tools allow being used as part of the modeling environment's integrated validation.

Chapter 5
Phase III: Generating Artifacts from the Model

A key benefit of a formal model is the possibility to derive artifacts from the mapping and the domain logic it captures. This section describes the scope of this approach, as well as the similarities evident in the artifacts of LDML.de.

In the process of generating artifacts, structures are selected from the mapping and translated into structures of the desired output artifact. The most common artifact types are technical (such as boilerplate code, data schemas, ontologies, and configuration files) or explanatory (specifications, visualizations, or summaries). Regardless of the artifact type, the generation process demands a technical definition of correspondences between structures in the formal model and the desired artifact.

The start of this process is to identify the said correspondences between input structures and output structures for each desired artifact. Initially, a mock-up of the envisioned artifact can be created. Structures in the artifact are then matched to model structures. If the aim is, for example, to generate an HTML specification from the model containing tabular summaries of logical units in the model, one first needs to determine which objects in the model require such a table in the specification. Then properties of those model objects are linked to properties of an HTML table. For example, one might require a table for each class object in a UML model with the class name as the table title, the class properties in individual rows, and a style based on stereotypes assigned to the class object. This matching process might reveal gaps in the modeling methodology if the domain information contained in the model is insufficient for finer differentiations necessary when generating artifacts. This insufficiency will then need to be remedied. Having validated the formal model simplifies the generation process significantly, as it narrowly defines what input a generator needs to expect.

Ideally, the correspondences between model input and artifact output should be documented before implementation to avoid getting locked into a specific technology. A simple table describing expected input structures and their corresponding output structures should be sufficient for most artifacts.

A. Flatt et al., *Model-Driven Development of Akoma Ntoso Application Profiles*, https://doi.org/10.1007/978-3-031-14132-4_5

After documenting the correspondences, a technical translation mechanism to implement the generator needs to be chosen. Many modeling tools offer dedicated reporting wizards and custom templates for artifact generation. More complex requirements call for custom-built generators, for example, using templating languages such as VTL (Velocity Templating Language) and jinja2 or XSLT (Extensible Stylesheet Language Transformations). Given the variety of suitable technologies, providing guidance on how to implement the generators themselves is outside the scope of this book.

Finally, the generated outputs will have to be validated against technical and domain requirements (see Sect. 4.3). While the development process is described linearly, its actual realization will likely be highly iterative and incremental. The entire development pipeline, from requirements to modeling rules and model content to generators and output artifacts, is refined throughout the development effort.

5.1 Technically Restricting the Akoma Ntoso Schema

In customizing AKN, the most important artifact is a technical manifestation of the application profile. AKN is itself technically defined by an XML schema. There are two ways to define more restrictive schema rules to this XML schema. The first is to add a layer of assertions using either XML Schema 1.1 xs:asserts or Schematron; the second is to work directly on the XML Schema Definition (XSD) itself.

Assertions are a feasible way to prescribe specific, narrow patterns. To widely restrict and re-define the hierarchical structure of legal documents, essentially mirroring an entire graph, this was not deemed suitable. For such a complex set of structural rules with many eventualities, assertions require complex rules that are hard to read and error-prone. If such profound restrictions of AKN are to be enforced in the schema, even the UNIBO Subschema Generator[1] is not well-suited to capture these demands as it codifies the desired subset using assertions.

The second option implements new rules directly in XSD, the same schema language used to define the hierarchical structure of legal documents in AKN itself. An existing XML schema can be restricted by one of the following three mechanisms: direct editing, re-definition, or the introduction of additional schemas for validation.[2]

- *Direct editing*: The base schema is adjusted and overwritten, wherever necessary, and then used to validate instance documents.

---

[1] See http://akn.web.cs.unibo.it/akgenerator/.

[2] In addition, AKN offers another mechanism for customization, namely, a set of generic elements that can be used for semantic markup of context-specific elements. These, however, are not suited to specify validation rules at a schema level.

- *Re-definition*: The xs:redefine directive allows schemas to include the base schema and then selectively overwrite individual data types.
- *Additional schemas*: This method creates a new, modified schema from the base schema (as in the first approach) but uses implementation logic to validate all instance documents against both the new schema and the old base schema.

These schema-based restrictions can later be extended by using assertion-based technologies such as Schematron rules or assertions provided in XML Schema 1.1.

5.2 Modeling Rules for the German Case Study

In order to describe and exemplify modeling rules for the generation of artifacts from the model, we subsequently describe modeling rules that were envisaged by the authors to be applicable to the illustrative case study. Generally speaking, a technical manifestation of an application profile of AKN should consist of one or more schemas that restrict the set of valid AKN instances to a subset in line with drafting guidelines all the while ensuring that every valid instance of the application profile is also a valid instance of the original AKN definition.

Direct editing is not guaranteed to result in a true subset of the base AKN schema. The xs:redefine mechanism is limited to overwriting XML complex types (xs:complexType) and not suited to differentiate between individual XML elements (xs:element) all given the same complex type. Therefore, the third approach suggests itself: An additional custom schema can be developed to be used alongside the original AKN schema. Furthermore, that schema file should be as structurally similar to the base AKN schema as possible. To this end, the latter should be surveyed for design patterns and schema structures. These are then matched to their equivalents in the model. Table 5.1 exemplifies possible matchings.

The UML model is technically represented using an XML vocabulary, as are other artifacts of the created application profile. XSLT is therefore perfectly suited to define the necessary transformations and generators to derive the standard artifacts from the domain model. Also note the similarity to the XÖV toolset for XML standards, which also uses XSLT as a transformation technology.

Table 5.1 Matching of model elements and schema elements, prefaceHeader and prefaceBody

Model element	Schema element
UML class	xs:complexType
UML abstract class	xs:complexType abstract="true"
UML property	xs:element
UML stereotype *(from AKN vocabulary)*	xs:element/@name
Collection of properties of a UML class	xs:sequence
Two or more specializations of a UML class	xs:extension

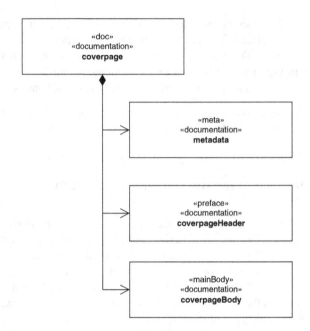

Fig. 5.1 UML class coverpage in the UML model

```
<xsd:complexType name="coverpage">
  <xsd:complexContent>
    <xsd:extension base="billDocument">
      <xsd:sequence>
        <xsd:element name="meta" type="metadata"/>
        <xsd:element name="preface" type="coverpageHeader"/>
        <xsd:element name="mainBody" type="coverpageBody"/>
      </xsd:sequence>
      <xsd:attributeGroup ref="doc"/>
    </xsd:extension>
  </xsd:complexContent>
</xsd:complexType>
```

Fig. 5.2 Corresponding xs:complexType in the generated XSD

Figures 5.1 and 5.2 exemplify this by showing a class in the UML model and its generated counterpart in XSD. The key logic shown here is one of conjunction: The object coverpage (recitals/preface) contains a sequence consisting of metadata.

Every class representing a legal object carries a UML stereotype "documentation" to hold domain-specific documentation, as well as at least one additional UML stereotype to indicate which AKN element is to be used to represent these objects in XML. Classes serving as technical constructs (for instance, for disjunctions or inheritance) are used without a stereotype denoting an AKN element, as these are not directly instantiated and exist to convey domain logic in the model.

Legal object	coverpage
AKN element	akn:doc
Documentation:	This structure is used for the independent coverpage belonging to a bill or act.
Generalizations	billDocument
Specializations	-
Used in	-

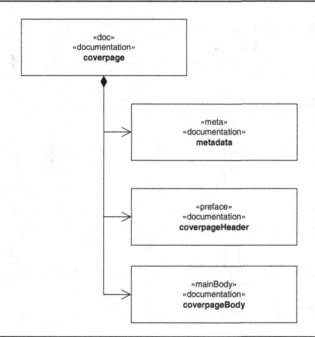

Child elements of *coverpage*			
Child element	**AKN element**	**Count.**	**Page**
metadata	*<meta>*	1	30
Metadata for the coverpage including bibliographical and editorial data and classifications.			
coverpageHeader	*<preface>*	1	42
Page header for the coverpage.			
coverpageBody	*<mainBody>*	1	234
Document body for the coverpage.			

Fig. 5.3 Example specification section corresponding to UML class coverpage

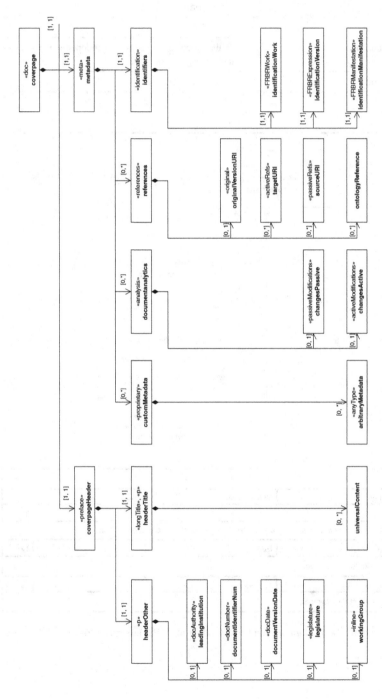

Fig. 5.4 Multi-level visualization of descendants of the structure coverpage

Consolidation and validation scripts can be used to reduce complexity in the transformation step and pinpoint inconsistencies and violations of modeling conventions in the model, narrowing down the variety of possible inputs the artifact generators have to handle.

A similar approach to the schema generation can be used in the generation of a specification document. In addition to the generation of schema components corresponding to a UML class, the UML model can be used to generate a specification section in the markup language DocBook for each UML class. As DocBook, too, is an XML format, the use of existing approaches around XSLT-based tools, namely, the KoSIT XÖV toolchain, is in the authors' opinion an obvious choice for the German use case.[3] Figure 5.3 showcases a specification section corresponding to the UML structure `coverpage` mentioned above.

In this example, the specification section created for each object contains an overview table that includes the object's non-technical name, the corresponding AKN element (in this instance `akn:doc`), its documentation, and details of its inheritance relationships to other objects. This is followed by a visualization, prescriptions on the object's usage, and, lastly, a tabular representation of the objects' content with references to their respective definitions in the specification. All of this content can be generated automatically from the UML model and is thus consistent with the remainder of the specification, the technical artifacts, and any visualization generated from the model.

Generators can also be used to produce various large-scale SVG visualizations of the legal structures contained in the formal model. These visualizations can serve as interactive, clickable presentation aids for stakeholder validation of the model or further use in the specification document (Fig. 5.4).

---

[3] See Koordinierungsstelle für ITStandards (2021) as well as http://www.xoev.de.

Chapter 6
Outlook and Lessons Learned

Legislative processes are characterized by a high degree of complexity and interdependence. This not only applies to the communication between the various actors involved but also to the content of a bill as well as the associated drafting and coordination processes. For fully digital legislative processes, it is therefore essential to establish common rules, procedures, and formats, e.g., on the basis of Akoma Ntoso between the actors involved. This will ensure that data and information are always interpreted in a uniform manner, even in the face of a heterogeneous IT landscape.

Akoma Ntoso needs to be adapted and specified for each use case by creating an application profile. This book describes a model-driven development approach for creating a national application profile for the international legislative markup of Akoma Ntoso. It also demonstrates the feasibility of this approach, as demonstrated in a case study of the German legislative system and the corresponding German application profile *LegalDocML.de*, that is based on this approach. The herein described model-driven development approach is advantageous because it ensures consistent and error-proof descriptive styles, even when using different software tools. It allows for easy maintenance, is self-documenting, and facilitates stakeholder validation with non-technical legal experts. The resulting application profile remains fully compliant to and compatible with Akoma Ntoso.

The book explains the motivation for such an application profile and describes its creation: An inventory of legal structures and a rudimentary mapping to AKN elements serve as a starting point for modeling the structure of the legal domain and AKN. The refinement of this rudimentary model to a formal model is necessary in order to obtain a complete and consistent model of the domain and its mapping to AKN. It is then described how this formal model can be used to generate technical and documentation artifacts for the application profile. A custom XML Schema Definition in addition to the AKN schema definition, generated using XSLT scripts, is found to be the most suitable way for the technical description of the application profile.

© The Author(s), under exclusive license to Springer Nature Switzerland AG 2022   39
A. Flatt et al., *Model-Driven Development of Akoma Ntoso Application Profiles*,
https://doi.org/10.1007/978-3-031-14132-4_6

Several conclusions can be drawn from this process:

On the subject of customizing AKN, a critical insight is that the standard's customization options are best suited for simple structural adjustments and not intended to be used for complex cross-level rule definitions. The AKN schema is designed to be adapted for specific use cases such as national or supranational legal systems. However, most mechanisms on offer are suitable only for small adjustments and restrictions such as defining nesting orders of hierarchical elements. Many of the design patterns realized in the AKN schema hardly lend themselves to large-scale customizations, as XSD group-like structures (such as `xs:group` and `xs:attributeGroup`) are pervasive and difficult to reconfigure.

Model-driven approaches to developing application profiles seem very promising. While this development approach requires significant upfront effort to develop and refine the methodology and toolchain, it can yield significant benefits. Firstly, the formal model is useful in validating requirements with stakeholders and iterating on their feedback. Secondly, the formal model serves as a single point of truth, storing and maintaining all information on the domain and the mapping. Thus, the initial effort can quickly be recouped when implementing changes to the model and artifacts. This is particularly relevant when taking into account the overall lifecycle of the application profile and the possibility of reusing the formal model to guide software development for applications implementing the application profile.

In order to realize these benefits, two qualities of the development team are indispensable: A robust understanding of the modeling language as well as of the structure of each desired output artifact is needed to design both specific modeling rules and the artifact generators. Moreover, the rules and methodology need to be communicated and documented in order to be followed consistently by the team members.

Many of the findings presented herein are transferable: The model-driven development approach is well-suited to perform extensive customization of XML schemas. As the need to formalize true subsets of existing XML schemas is expected to arise in any number of domains, this presents an opportunity to design a generic framework for model-based customizations. In order to generalize the process to a framework for subschema generation, the UML-based development approach described in this book suggests further research and work regarding a number of issues: For instance, the aspects of an XML schema that a UML profile needs to account for in order to ensure a suitable model should be systematized. This includes data structures such as `xs:choice` and `xs:sequence` as well as mechanisms such as inheritance, but needs to be investigated further for completeness.

Similarly, it would be desirable to provide a mechanism for formally proving a generated subschema's conformance with the base schema, removing the necessity to additionally validate against the base schema. Furthermore, other potential reuses of the formal model, for example, as the basis of additional artifacts, should be investigated.

Bibliography

Barabucci, G., et al. (2011). Long-term preservation of legal resources. In K.N Andersen et al. (Eds.), *Electronic government and the information systems perspective*. EGOVIS 2011 Lecture notes in computer science (Vol. 6866, pp. 78–93). Springer. https://dl.acm.org/doi/abs/10.5555/2033665.2033675

Bernauer, M., Kappel, G., & Kramler, G. (2004). Representing XML schema in UML—a comparison of approaches. In M.W Nora Koch Piero Fraternali (Ed.), *International Conference on Web Engineering, vol. 4th International Conference, ICWE 2004, Munich, Germany July26–30, Proceedings* (pp. 440–444). Springer. https://doi.org/10.1007/978-3-540-27834-4_54

Beydeda, S., Book, M., & Gruhn, V. (Eds.). (2005). *Model—driven software development*. Springer. https://doi.org/10.1007/354028554-7

Boella, G., et al. (2014). *European and National Legislation and case law linked in open data stack—D2.2 legal XML-schema (XSD)*.

Boella, G., et al. (2015). Linking legal open data. In T. Sichelman, & K. Atkinson (Eds.), *Proceedings of the 15th International Conference on Artificial Intelligence and Law*. ACM. https://doi.org/10.1145/2746090.2746106

Brunn, B. (2004). Möglichkeiten einer Rechtsförmlichkeitsprüfung im parlamentarischen Verfahren. In *Zeitschrift für Rechtspolitik* (pp. 79–81).

Bumke, C., & Voßkuhle, A. (2019). *German constitutional law*. Oxford University Press. https://doi.org/10.1093/law/9780198808091.001.0001

Bundesministerium der Justiz. (2008). *Handbuch der Rechtsförmlichkeit, 3. Auflage*, Bundesministerium der Justiz. https://hdr.bmj.de/

Bundesministerium der Justiz. (2022). *Das neue Rechtsinformationsportal—Schaffung eines einheitlichen und modernen Zugangs zu Rechtsinformationen des Bundes*. Press Release. https://www.bmj.de/DE/Ministerium/Transparenz/Rechtsinformationsportal/Rechtsinformationsportal.html (visited on: 04/20/2021).

Bundesministerium des Innern, für Bau und Heimat, Projektgruppe Digitale Verwaltung 2020, Projektgruppe Gemeinsame IT des Bundes. (2016). *Erster Newsletter der eGesetzgebung*. Newsletter. https://www.verwaltung-innovativ.de/SharedDocs/Publikationen/Gesetzgebung/erster_newsletter.pdf?__blob=publicationFile&v=3 (visited on: 04/20/2021).

Bundesministerium des Innern, für Bau und Heimat, Projektgruppe Digitale Verwaltung 2020, Projektgruppe Gemeinsame IT des Bundes. (2017). *Dritter Newsletter der eGesetzgebung*. Newsletter. https://www.verwaltunginnovativ.de/SharedDocs/Publikationen/Gesetzgebung/dritter_newsletter.pdf?__blob=publicationFile&v=3 (visited on: 04/20/2021).

Bundesministerium des Innern, für Bau und Heimat, Projektgruppe Digitale Verwaltung 2020, Projektgruppe Gemeinsame IT des Bundes. (2019a). *Vierter Newsletter der eGesetzgebung*

Newsletter der eGesetzgebung. Newsletter. https://www.verwaltung-innovativ.de/SharedDocs/
Publikationen/Gesetzgebung/vitter_newsletter_q2_2019.pdf?__blob=publicationFile&v=4
(visited on: 04/20/2021).

Bundesministerium des Innern, für Bau und Heimat, Projektgruppe Digitale Verwaltung
2020, Projektgruppe Gemeinsame IT des Bundes. (2019b). *Vorstellung der E-
Gesetzgebung.* Presentation. https://www.verwaltung-innovativ.de/SharedDocs/Publikationen/
Gesetzgebung/projektdarstellung_e_gesetzgebung.pdf?__blob=publicationFile&v=8   (visited
on: 04/20/2021).

Bundesministerium des Innern, für Bau und Heimat, Projektgruppe Digitale Verwaltung 2020,
Projektgruppe Gemeinsame IT des Bundes. (2020). *Fünfter Newsletter der eGesetzgebung.*
Newsletter.   https://www.verwaltung-innovativ.de/SharedDocs/Publikationen/Gesetzgebung/f
%C3%BCnfter_newsletter.pdf?__blob=publicationFile&v=6 (visited on: 04/20/2021).

Bundesministerium des Innern, für Bau und Heimat, Projektgruppe Digitale Verwaltung
2020, Projektgruppe Gemeinsame IT des Bundes. (2021a). *Sechster Newsletter der
eGesetzgebung.* Newsletter. https://www.verwaltunginnovativ.de/SharedDocs/Publikationen/
Gesetzgebung/sechster_newsletter.pdf?__blob=publicationFile&v=5 (visited on: 04/20/2021).

Bundesministerium des Innern, für Bau und Heimat, Projektgruppe Digitale Verwaltung
2020, Projektgruppe Gemeinsame IT des Bundes. (2021b). *Siebter Newsletter der
eGesetzgebung.* Newsletter. https://www,verwaltung-innovativ.de/SharedDocs/Publikationen/
Gesetzgebung/siebter_newsletter.pdf?__blob=publicationFile&v=7 (visited on: 04/20/2021).

Bundesministerium des Innern, für Bau und Heimat, Projektgruppe Digitale Verwaltung 2020,
Projektgruppe Gemeinsame IT des Bundes. (2021c). *Website of the project E-legislation.* http://
egesetzgebung.bund.de/index.html (visited on: 04/20/2021).

Bundesministerium des Innern, für Bau und Heimat, Projektgruppe Digitale Verwaltung 2020,
Projektgruppe Gemeinsame IT des Bundes. (2021d). *Website of the Standard LegalDocML.de
within the project E-legislation.* http://egesetzgebung.bund.de/legaldocml.html (visited on:
04/20/2021).

Büttner, F., et al. (2014). Model-driven standardization of public authority data interchange.
Science of Computer Programming, 89, 162–175. https://doi.org/10.1016/j.scico.2013.03.009

Deutsch, A. (2017). Schriftlichkeit im Recht: Kommunikationsformen und Textsorten. In E. Felder
& F. Vogel (Eds.), *Handbuch Sprache im Recht*, (pp. 91–117) De Gruyter. https://doi.org/10.
1515/9783110296198-005

Deutscher Bundestag. (2020). *Antwort der Bundesregierung auf die Kleine Anfrage der Fraktion
DIE LINKE, Drucksache 19/25438.* Deutscher Bundestag. https://dserver.bundestag.de/btd/19/
256/1925654.pdf

Dimyadi, J., Governatori, G., & Amor, R. (2017). Evaluating LegalDocML and LegalRuleML as
a standard for sharing normative information in the AEC/FM domain. In F. Bosché, I. Brilakis,
& R. Sacks (Eds.), *Lean and Computing in Construction Congress—Volume 1: Proceedings of
the Joint Conference on Computing in Construction.* Heriot-Watt University. https://doi.org/10.
24928/JC32017/0012

Dolin, R. (2021). XML in law: The role of standards in legal informatics. In D.M. Katz, R. Dolin,
& M.J. Bommarito (Eds.), *Legal informatics* (pp. 61–68). Cambridge University Press. https://
doi.org/10.1017/9781316529683.007

Dominguez, E., et al. (2007). A survey of UML models to XML schemas transformations.
In B. Benatallah et al. (Eds.), *Web Information Systems Engineering—WISE 2007, vol. 8th
International Conference on Web Information Systems Engineering* (pp. 184–195). Springer.
https://doi.org/10.1007/978-3-540-76993-4_16

Dominguez, E., et al. (2011). Evolution of XML schemas and documents from stereotyped UML
class models: A traceable approach. *Information and Software Technology, 53*(1), 34–50.
https://doi.org/10.1016/j.infsof.2010.08.001

Döring, M., & Noack, S. (2020). Standardisierter Datenaustausch. In: T. Klenk, F. Nullmeier, &
G. Wewer (Eds.), *Handbuch Digitalisierung in Staat und Verwaltung* (pp. 633–643). Springer
Fachmedien Wiesbaden. https://doi.org/10.1007/978-3-658-23668-7_59

Felder, E., & Vogel, F.. (2017). *Handbuch Sprache im Recht*. De Gruyter. https://doi.org/10.1515/9783110296198

Francesconi, E. (2022). The winter the summer and the summer dream of artificial intelligence in law. In *Artificial intelligence and law*. https://doi.org/10.1007/s10506-022-09309-8

Gen, K., et al. (2016). Applying the Akoma Ntoso XML schema to Japanese legislation. *Journal of Law Information & Science, 24*(2), 49–70. https://search.informit.org/doi/10.3316/ielapa.556807524334387

Hamann, H. (2014). Redaktionsversehen: Ein Beitrag zur Legislativfehlerlehre und zur Rechtsförmlichkeit. In *Archiv des öffentlichen Rechts* (pp. 446–475). https://doi.org/10.1628/000389114X14104459599689

Heeger, V. (2021). *E-Gesetzgebung: Wann kommt das Super-Tool?*, Article. https://background.tagesspiegel.de/digitalisierung/e-gesetzgebung-wann-kommt-das-super-tool (visited on: 04/20/2021).

Joshi, A., et al. (2021). A knowledge organization system for the United Nations sustainable development goals. In R. Verborgh et al. (Eds.), *The semantic web* (pp. 548–564). Springer International Publishing. https://doi.org/10.1007/978-3-030-77385-4_33.

Kahlert, A. (2014). Rechtsgestaltung mit der Methode KORA. *Datenschutz und Datensicherheit-DuD, 38*(2), 86–92. https://doio.rg/10.1007/s11623-014-0038-4

Kirchhof, G. (2009). *Die Allgemeinheit des Gesetzes über einen notwendigen Garanten der Freiheit, der Gleichheit und der Demokratie*. Mohr Siebeck. https://doi.org/10.1628/978-3-16-151265-0

Kluth, W., & Krings, G. (2013). *Gesetzgebung Rechtsetzung durch Parlamente und Verwaltungen sowie ihre gerichtliche Kontrolle*. C.F Müller Wissenschaft.

Koniaris, M., Papastefanatos, G., & Vassiliou, Y. (2016). Towards automatic structuring and semantic indexing of legal documents. In *Proceedings of the 20th Pan-Hellenic Conference on Informatics*. ACM. https://doi.org/10.1145/3003733.3003801

Leps, O. (2016). *Nutzung und Akzeptanz von E-Government-Fachanwendungen in der öffentlichen Verwaltung: Eine empirische Analyse am Beispiel des europäischen Binnenmarkt-Informationssystems*. Logos.

Leventis, S., Anastasiou, V., & Fitsilis, F. (2020). Application of enterprise integration patterns for the digital transformation of parliamentary control. In *Proceedings of the 13th International Conference on Theory and Practice of Electronic Governance, ICEGOV 2020, , Athens, Greece* (pp. 738–741) Association for Computing Machinery. https://doi.org/10.1145/3428502.3428612

Loutsaris, M.A., & Charalabidis, Y. (2020). Legal informatics from the aspect of interoperability: A review of systems, tools and ontologies. In *Proceedings of the 13th International Conference on Theory and Practice of Electronic Governance, ICEGOV 2020, Athens, Greece* (pp. 731–737). Association for Computing Machinery. https://doi.org/10.1145/3428502.3428611

Mens, T., & Gorp, P. V. (2006). A taxonomy of model transformation. *Electronic Notes in Theoretical Computer Science, 152*, 125–142. https://doi.org/10.1016/j.entcs.2005.10.021

Moreno Schneider, J., et al. (2022). Lynx: A knowledge-based AI service platform for content processing, enrichment and analysis for the legal domain. *Information Systems, 106*, 101966. https://doi.org/10.1016/j.is.2021.101966

Normenkontrollrat, N. (2019). *Erst der Inhalt, dann die Paragrafen. Gesetze wirksam und praxistauglich gestalten* (pp. 125–142). Nationaler Normenkontrollrat. https://www.normenkontrollrat.bund.de/nkr-de/service/publikationen/gutachten-und-positionspapiere/nkr-gutachten-2019-erst-der-inhalt-dann-die-paragrafen--1680554.

Ostendorff, M., Blume, T, & Ostendorff, S. (2020), Towards an open platform for legal information. In *Proceedings of the ACM/IEEE Joint Conference on Digital Libraries in 2020* (pp. 385–388). IEEE. https://doi.org/10.4855/arXiv.2005.13342

Palmirani, M. (2019). Akoma Ntoso for making FAO resolutions accessible. In G. Peruginelli & S. Faro (Eds.), *Knowledge of the law in the big data age* (pp. 159–169). IOS Press. https://doi.org/10.3233/FAIA190018

Palmirani, M. (2021). Lexdatafication: Italian legal knowledge modelling in Akoma Ntoso. In V
Rodriguez-Doncel et al. (Eds.), *AI approaches to the complexity of legal systems XI-XII* (pp.
31–47). Springer. https://doi.org/10.1007/978-3-030-89811-3_3

Palmirani, M., & Brighi, R. (2010). Model regularity of legal language in active modifications. In
P. Casanovas et al. (Eds.), *AI approaches to the complexity of legal systems. complex systems,
the semantic web, ontologies, argumentation, and dialogue. International Workshops AICOL-
I IVR-XXIV Beijing, China, September 19, 2009 and AICOL-II JURIX 2009*, Rotterdam, The
Netherlands, December 16, 2009 Revised Selected Papers (pp. 54–73). Springer. https://doi.
org/10.1007/978-3-642-16524-5_5

Palmirani, M., & Vitali, F. (2011). Akoma-Ntoso for legal documents. In G. Sartor et al. (Eds.),
Legislative XML for the semantic web (pp. 75–100). Springer. https://doi.org/10.1007/978-94-
007-1887-6_6

Palmirani, M., & Vitali, F. (2012). *Legislative XML: Principles and technical tools*, Inter-American
Development Bank.

Palmirani, M., et al. (2021). Hybrid AI framework for legal analysis of the EU legislation
corrigenda. In *Legal knowledge and information systems* (pp. 68–75). IOS Press. https://doi.
org/10.3233/FAIA210319

Piesker A., Schweizer, P, & Steffens, C. (2020). Elektronische Gesetzgebung. In T. Klenk, F.
Nullmeier, & G. Wewer (Eds.), *Handbuch Digitalisierung in Staat und Verwaltung* (pp. 633–
643). Springer Fachmedien Wiesbaden. https://doi.org/10.1007/978-3-658-23668-7_27.

Sannier, N., et al. (2017). Legal markup generation in the large: An experience report. In *2017
IEEE 25th International Requirements Engineering Conference (RE)*. IEEE. https://doi.org/10.
1109/RE.2017.10

Sansone, C., & Sperli, G. (2022). Legal information retrieval systems: State-of-the-art and open
issues. *Information Systems, 106*, 101967. https://doi.org/10.1016/j.is.2021.101967

Sartor, G. (2016). Open management of legislative documents. In C. Stefanou & H. Xanthaki
(Eds.), *Drafting legislation a modern approach* (pp. 259–286). Routledge.

Sartor, G., et al. (Eds.). (2011). *Legislative XML for the semantic web*. Springer. https://doi.org/10.
1007/978-94-007-1887-6

Schneider J., M. et al. (2022). Lynx: A knowledge-based AI service platform for content
processing, enrichment and analysis for the legal domain. *Information Systems, 106*, 101966.
https://doi.org/10.1016/j.is.2021.101966

Semsrott, A. (2020). *Best of Informationsfreiheit: Gesetze im Internet—aber bitte richtig!*. Article.
https://www.heise.de/meinung/Best-of-Informationsfreiheit-Gesetze-im-Internet-aber-bitte-
richtig-4937622.html (visited on: 04/20/2021).

Smeddinck, U. (2013). Gesetzgebungsmethodik und Gesetzestypen In W. Kluth & G. Krings
(Eds.), *Gesetzgebung Rechtsetzung durch Parlamente und Verwaltungen sowie ihre gerichtliche
Kontrolle* (pp. 69–94). C.F Müller Wissenschaft.

Stavropoulou, S., et al. (2020). Architecting an innovative big open legal data analytics, search
and retrieval platform. In *Proceedings of the 13th International Conference on Theory and
Practice of Electronic Governance, ICEGOV 2020, Athens, Greece* (pp. 723–730). Association
for Computing Machinery. https://doi.org/10.1145/3428502.3428610

Sutherland, S. (2022). *Legal data and information in practice: How data and the law interact*.
Taylor & Francis.

Thieme, S., & Raff, G. (2017). Verständlichkeit von Gesetzestexten und ihre Optimierung in der
Praxis. In E. Felder & F. Vogel (Eds.), *Handbuch Sprache im Recht* (pp. 391–424). De Gruyter.
https://doi.org/10.1515/9783110296198-020

Vergottini, G. (2018). *The pocket guide to Akoma Ntoso* (2nd ed.). Xcential Corpora-
tion. https://www.oasis-open.org/committees/download.php/62993/The%20Pocket%20Guide
%20to%20Akoma%20Ntoso%20-%202nd%20Edition.docx

Vitali, F, & Palmirani, M. (2019). Akoma Ntoso: Flexibility and customization to meet different
legal traditions. In S. Bauman (Ed.), *Proceedings of the Symposium on Markup Vocabulary Customization* (Vol. 24). Mulberry Technologies. https://doi.org/10.4242/balisagevol24.
palmirani01

Vitali, F., & Zeni, F. (2007). Towards a country–independent data format: The Akoma Ntoso experience. In C. Biagioli, E. Francesconi, & G. Sartor (Eds.), *Proceedings of the V Legislative XML Workshop*. European Press Academic Publishing.

Waltl, B., & Matthes, F. (2014). Towards measures of complexity: Applying structural and linguistic metrics to German laws. In *JURIX - legal knowledge and information systems*. IOP Press. https://doi.org/10.3233/978-1-61499-468-8-153

Weckerling-Wilhelm, D. (2013). Zu den Anforderungen der Rechtsförmlichkeit. In W. Kluth & G. Krings (Eds.), *Gesetzgebung Rechtsetzung durch Parlamente und Verwaltungen sowie ihre gerichtliche Kontrolle* (pp. 247–278). C.F Müller Wissenschaft.

Standards and Norms

Bundesministerium der Justiz und für Verbraucherschutz. (2020). *xNorm, version 1.0.2.* https://www.xrepository.de/details/urn:xoev-de:bmjv:standard:xnorm

Bundesministerium des Innern, für Bau und Heimat. (2020). *Spezifikation LegalDocML.de—XML-Standard für Dokumente der Bundesrechtsetzung, Fassung vom 27.03.2020, Version 1.0.* https://fragdenstaat.de/a/202866

Koordinierungsstelle für ITStandards. (2021). *Handbuch zur Entwicklung XÖV-konformer Standards, Version 2.4 | Fassung vom 15. Dezember 2021.* https://www.xoev.de/de/handbuch

Object Management Group. (2017). *Unified modeling language (UML), version 2.5.1, OMG.* https://www.omg.org/spec/UML/2.5.1/

Organization for the Advancement of Structured Information Standards. (2018). *Akoma Ntoso Version 1.0 Part 1: XML Vocabulary Edited by Monica Palmirani, Roger Sperberg, Grant Vergottini, and Fabio Vitali, 29 August 2018. OASIS Standard,* http://docs.oasis-open.org/legaldocml/akn-core/v1.0-os-part1-vocabulary/akn-core-v1.0/os/part1-vocabulary.html. Latestversion: http://docs.oasis-open.org/legaldocml/akn-core/v1.0/akn-core-v1.0-part1-vocabulary.html, http://docs.oasis-open.org/legaldocml/

Organization for the Advancement of Structured Information Standards. (2019a). *Electronic court filing version 5.0, committee specification 01, 18 April 2019.* https://docs.oasis-open.org/legalxmlcourtfiling/

Organization for the Advancement of Structured Information Standards. (2019b). *Litigant portal exchange version 1.0, committee specification draft 01/public review draft 01, 06 August 2019.* https://docs.oasis-open.org/lp/

Organization for the Advancement of Structured Information Standards. (2021a). *DocBook specification v. 4.5.* https://www.oasis-open.org/docbook/specs/

Organization for the Advancement of Structured Information Standards. (2021b). *LegalRuleML core specification version 1.0, OASIS standard, 30 August 2021.* http://docs.oasis-open.org/legalruleml/

Publications Office of the European Union. (2020). *Akoma Ntoso for EU (AKN4EU), version 3.0.* http://publications.europa.eu/resource/dataset/akn4eu

The [UK] National Archives. (2019). *Crown legislation markup language.* https://www.legislation.gov.uk/

United Nations System, Chief Executives Board for Coordination, High-Level Committee on Management (HLCM). (2020). *Akoma Ntoso for the United Nations System, Guidelines for the mark-up of UN normative, parliamentary and judicial documents.* https://www.w3id.org/un/schema/akn4un/

© The Author(s), under exclusive license to Springer Nature Switzerland AG 2022   47
A. Flatt et al., *Model-Driven Development of Akoma Ntoso Application Profiles,*
https://doi.org/10.1007/978-3-031-14132-4

Printed in the United States
by Baker & Taylor Publisher Services